YOU ARE

awesome

adults coloring book with motivation words for relax and stress relieve

this coloring book
belongs to

____

color test page

My dream
My future

Your soul
is full of
SUNSHINE

HAPPY
IS THE
new
RICH

COLORING BOOK

You Are
Capable
Of Amazing
Things

Always
Start
Your Day
With
A Cup
Of
Positivitea

TODAY
ANYTHING IS
Possible

Be Kind

COLORING BOOK

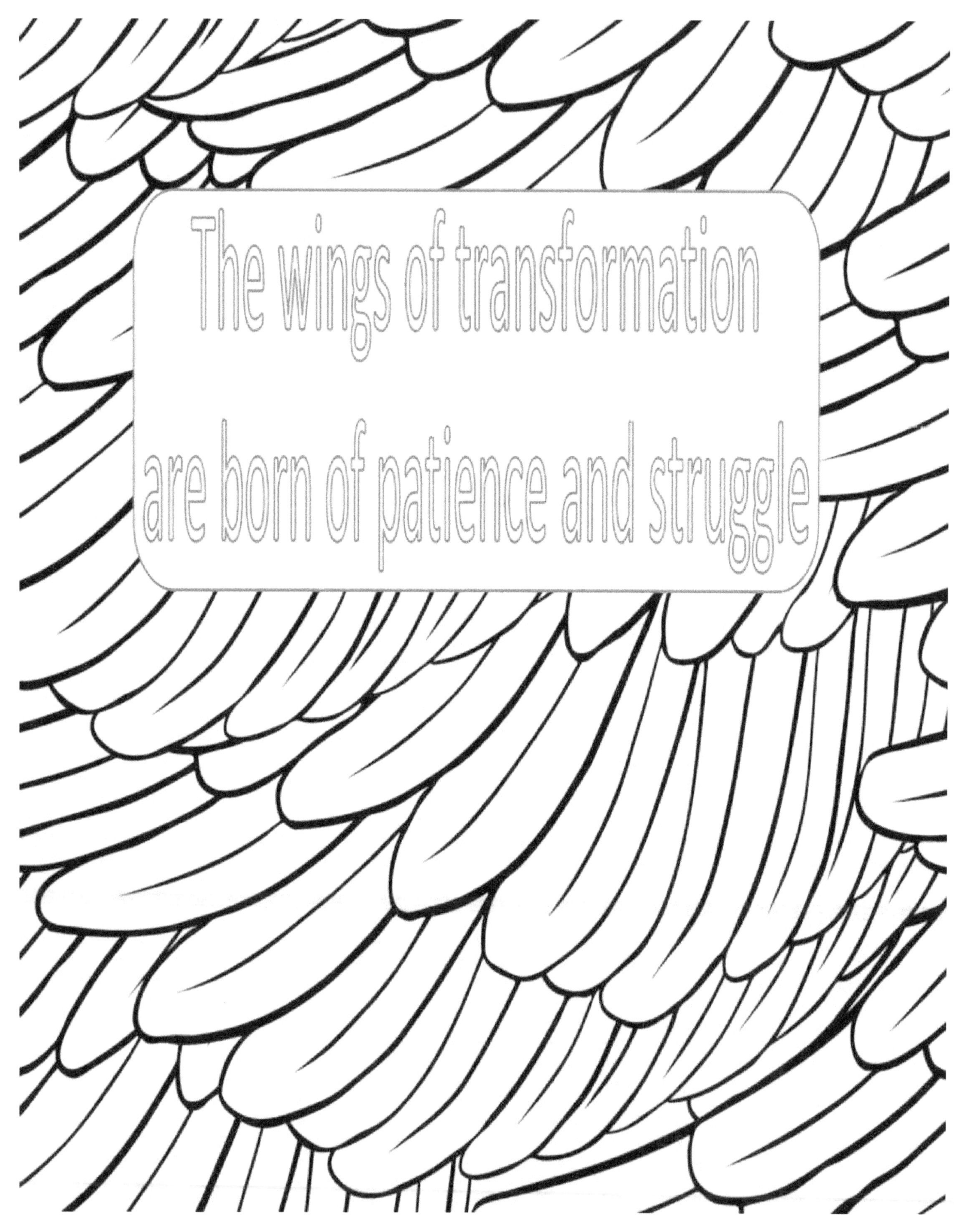

The wings of transformation
are born of patience and struggle

COLORING BOOK

DREAM BIG
WORK HARD

COLORING BOOK

Life Is A Miracle Enjoy The Ride

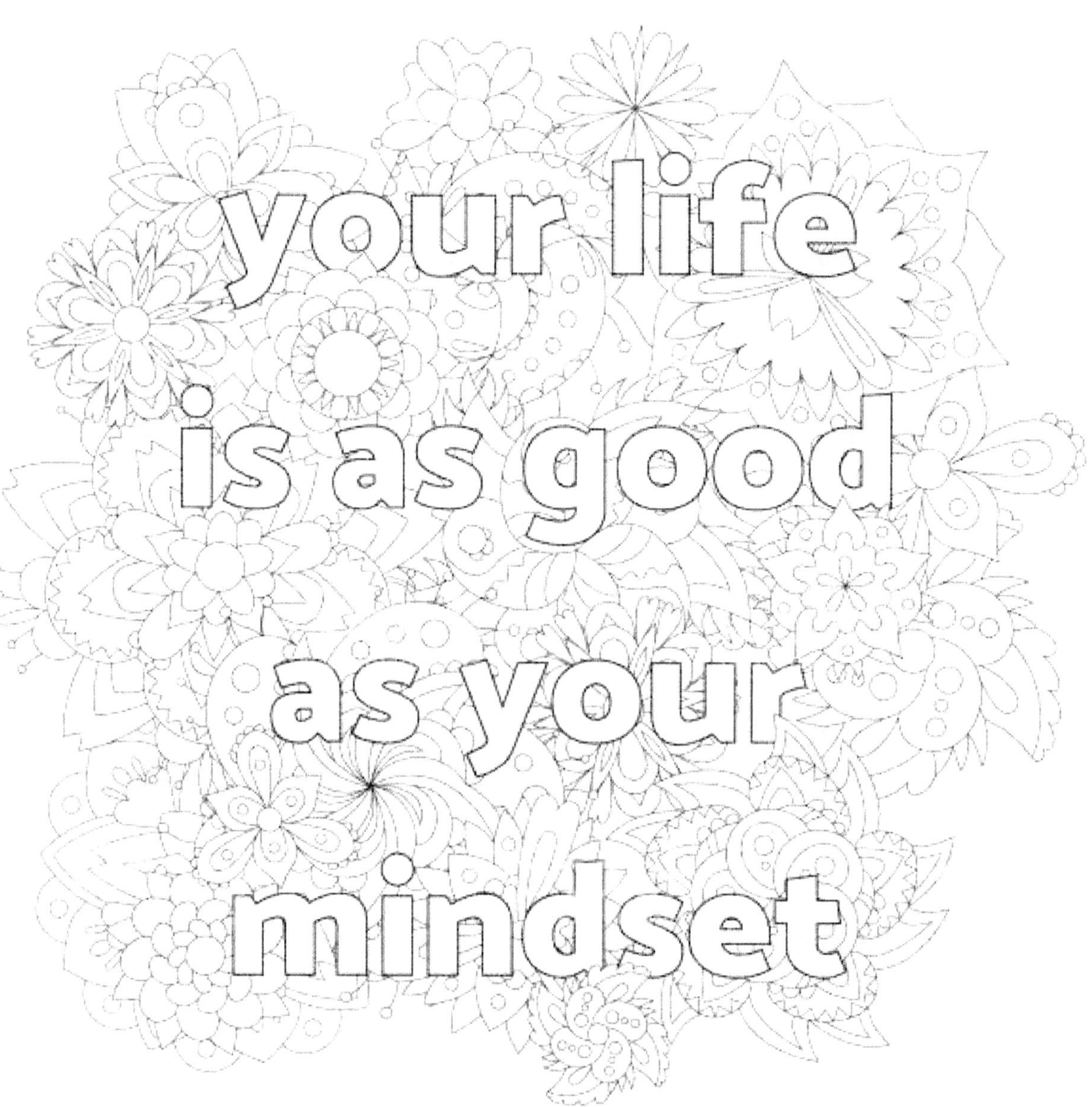
your life
is as good
as your
mindset

COLORING BOOK

Escape
The
Ordinary

Keep Calm
& Have
Boundaries

Select
you
Size

Your Limitation - It's Only Your Imagination

Let
Go
of the
Thoughts
That
Don't
Make
You
Strong

COLORING BOOK

Your
soul
is
GOLDEN

Great
Things
Rarely
Come From
Comfort
Zones

Dream It.
Wish It.
Do It.

Do What
Makes
Your Soul
Shine

COLORING BOOK

Keep Calm
& Have
Boundaries

COLORING BOOK

Make
Yourself
PROUD

Hippie

COLORING BOOK

Limit Your "Always" And Your "Nevers"
Amy Poehler

COLORING BOOK

ALL BODIES
ARE GOOD
BODIES

Do Something
Today That
Your Future
Self Will
Thank You
For

"Believe You Can And You're Halfway There."
Theodore Roosevelt

Sometimes
We're Tested
Not To Show
Our
Weaknesses,
But To
Discover Our
Strengths

Dream It.
Wish It.
Do It.

COLORING BOOK

Do What
Makes
Your Soul
Shine

"Hard work keeps the wrinkles out of the mind and spirit."
— Helena Rubinstein.

TRUST

Reach for your Dreams.
The Universe will Rise to meet them.

Remember, YOU teach people how to treat you.

Reach for your Dreams.
The Universe will Rise to meet them.

LOVE

BEAUTY

COLORING BOOK

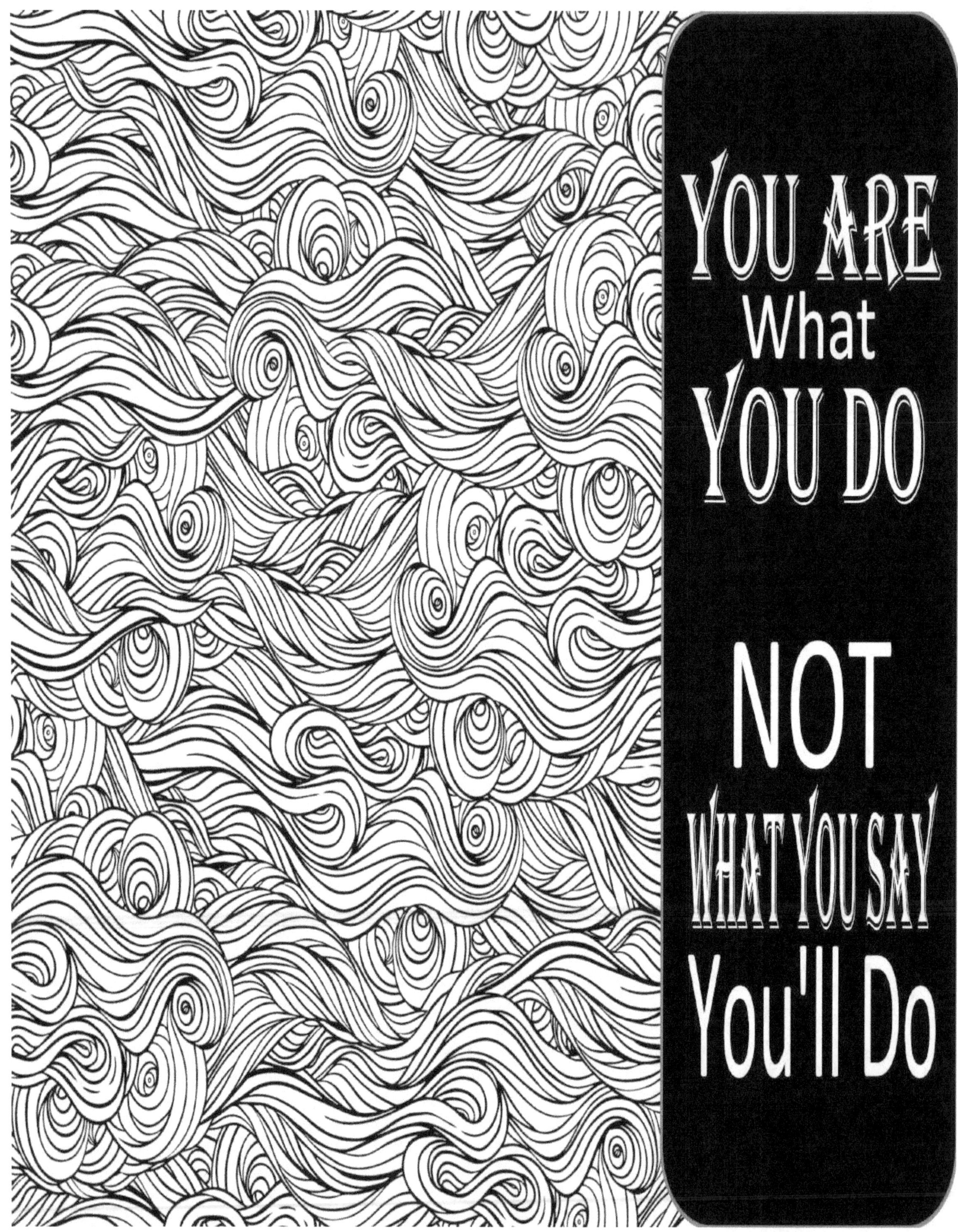

YOU ARE
What
YOU DO

NOT
WHAT YOU SAY
You'll Do

I AM
LIMITLESS

Perfectly
Imperfect

Friends
DON'T LET
FRIENDS
trash
the
world

COLORING BOOK

Make
Yourself
A
Priority

Make
Yourself
a
priority

Stop
Wishing
Start
Doing

IT'S
NEVER
too LATE
TO LOSE
that
weight

Make Your
Own
Magic

dream
believe
achieve

Anything
Possible

I've Got
This

COLORING BOOK

Dream.
Plan.
Do.

The Key To Success Is To Focus On Goals, Not Obstacles.

YOU
ARE
THE
BEST

Keep
Life
simple

Enjoy
Life

Unlock your POTENTIAL

Great Things
Rarely Come
From
Comfort
Zones

COLORING BOOK

I'M NOT
perfect,
BUT I AM
LIMITED
AM
edition

SO
much
WORLD
SO little
TIME

YES YOU
CAN

Life is short, and
it is up to you
to make it sweet. -
Sarah Louise Delany

MAKE
MAGIC
TODAY

Do
Something
Today That
Your Future
Self Will
Thank You
For

I CAN   AND   I WILL

COLORING BOOK

be happy

The ONLY time you should ever look back is to see how far you've come.

being

DIFFERENT

is your

SUPERPOWER

Dream It.
Wish It.
Do It.

If You Know Better Then, Do Better

BE
YOUR
OWN
MUSE

COLORING BOOK

I value
MYSELF

COLORING BOOK

You're
a GEM

Glitter
Is Always
An Option

Let go
of what
you can't
CHANGE